3 Section Page Storyboard Book

Copyright 2018 - SquarePort Studio

ISBN-13: 978-1724727787

ISBN-10: 1724727788

Notes - Scribbles - Anything Else

Notes - Scribbles - Anything Else

Notes - Scribbles - Anything Else

Notes - Scribbles - Anything Else

Notes - Scribbles - Anything Else

Notes - Scribbles - Anything Else

Notes - Scribbles - Anything Else

Notes - Scribbles - Anything Else

Notes - Scribbles - Anything Else

Notes - Scribbles - Anything Else

Notes - Scribbles - Anything Else

Notes - Scribbles - Anything Else

Notes - Scribbles - Anything Else

Notes - Scribbles - Anything Else

Notes - Scribbles - Anything Else

Notes - Scribbles - Anything Else

Notes - Scribbles - Anything Else

Notes - Scribbles - Anything Else

Notes - Scribbles - Anything Else

Notes - Scribbles - Anything Else

Notes - Scribbles - Anything Else

Notes - Scribbles - Anything Else

Notes - Scribbles - Anything Else

Notes - Scribbles - Anything Else

Notes - Scribbles - Anything Else

Notes - Scribbles - Anything Else

Notes - Scribbles - Anything Else

Notes - Scribbles - Anything Else

Notes - Scribbles - Anything Else

Notes - Scribbles - Anything Else

Notes - Scribbles - Anything Else

Notes - Scribbles - Anything Else

Notes - Scribbles - Anything Else

Notes - Scribbles - Anything Else

Notes - Scribbles - Anything Else

Notes - Scribbles - Anything Else

Notes - Scribbles - Anything Else

SquarePort Studio